Emma Edmonds The Great Hero And Spy Of The Civil War

The Incredible True Life Story Of Emma Sarah Edmonds The Great Hero And Spy Of The Civil War

Confidence Adaeze

Table of Contents

CHAPTER ONE 3

   December 1841 – September 5, 1898 3

CHAPTER TWO 13

   Sarah Emma Edmond As A Youth 13

   Sarah Emma Edmonds in the Civil War:........15

CHAPTER THREE 29

   Sarah Emma Edmonds After the Civil War...29

CHAPTER FOUR 40

   Sarah Emma Edmonds - Civil War Warrior, Spy, and Medical caretaker...........................40

   THE END 49

CHAPTER ONE

December 1841 – September 5, 1898

Sarah Emma Edmondson was conceived in New Brunswick, Canada in December 1841. Her dad was a rancher who had been seeking after a child to assist him with the harvests; thus, he despised his little girl and abused her. In 1857, to get away from the maltreatment and a masterminded marriage, Edmondson ventured out from home, changing her name to Edmonds.

Edmonds lived and worked in the town of Moncton for about a year, yet consistently frightful that she would be found by her dad, she chose to move to the US. To head out undetected and to make sure about a work, she chose to mask herself as a man and took the name Franklin Thompson. She before long looked for some kind of employment in Hartford, Connecticut as a voyaging Book of scriptures sales rep.

By the beginning of the Common Battle in 1861, Edmonds was boarding in Stone, Michigan, proceeding to be very fruitful at selling books. A vigorous Unionist, she concluded that the most ideal approach to help is to enroll under her moniker, and on May 25, 1861, Edmonds was gathered into the second Michigan Infantry as a long term enlist.

In spite of the fact that Edmonds and her confidants didn't partake in the Skirmish of First Manassas on July 21, they were instrumental in covering the Association retreat from the field. Edmonds remained behind to nurture injured troopers and scarcely escaped being caught from her revisitations of her regiment in Washington. She kept on functioning as a medical clinic specialist for the following a while.

In Spring of 1862, Edmonds was allocated the obligations of mail transporter for the regiment. Soon thereafter, the second Michigan was transported out to Virginia as a component of General McClellan's Promontory Mission. From April 5 to May 4, the regiment partook in the Attack of Yorktown.

It was during this time that Edmonds was evidently first requested to lead undercover work missions. Despite the fact that there is no complete evidence that Edmonds ever gone about as a government operative, her diaries detail a few of her endeavors behind foe lines all through the war, camouflaged differently as a male "stash"and an Irish vendor.

On May 5, 1862, the regiment went under hefty fire during the Skirmish of Williamsburg. Edmonds was trapped in a tough situation, at one point getting a gun and discharging with her companions. She additionally went about as a cot conveyor, shipping the injured from the field for a really long time in the heavy storm.

The late spring of 1862 saw Edmonds proceeding with her part as a mail transporter, which frequently elaborate excursions of more than 100 miles through domain possessed by hazardous "bushwhackers."Edmonds'

regiment saw activity in the skirmishes of Reasonable Oaks and Malvern Slope, where she acted by and by as medical clinic orderly, keeping an eye on the many injured. With the halt of the Landmass Lobby, Edmonds got back with her regiment to Washington.

On August 29, 1862, the second Michigan partook in the Clash of Second Manassas. Going about as dispatch during the fight, Edmunds had to ride a donkey after her pony was slaughtered.

She was tossed into a jettison, breaking her leg and enduring inner wounds. These wounds would torment her for an amazing remainder and were the principle explanation behind her annuity application after the war.

During the Clash of Fredericksburg on December 11-15, Edmonds filled in as a deliberate for her officer, Colonel Orlando Poe. While her regiment didn't see a lot of activity, Edmonds was continually in the seat, handing off messages and requests from central command to the cutting edges.

In the spring of 1863, Edmonds and the second Michigan were relegated to the Multitude of the Cumberland and shipped off to Kentucky. Edmonds contracted jungle fever and mentioned a leave of absence, which was denied. Not having any desire to look for clinical consideration from the military because of a paranoid fear of revelation, Edmonds left her friends in middle April, never to return. "Franklin Thompson" was in this manner accused of renunciation.

After her recuperation, Edmonds, no longer in camouflage, worked with the US Christian Commission as a female medical attendant, from June 1863 until the finish of the war. She composed and distributed her journals, Medical caretaker and Spy in the Association Armed force, the primary version being delivered in 1864. Edmonds gave the benefits from her book to different warriors' guide gatherings.

Edmonds wedded Linus Seelye in 1867 and they had three youngsters. In 1876, she went to a gathering of the second Michigan and was heartily gotten by her confidants, who helped her in having the charge of departure eliminated from her military records and upheld her application for a military annuity. Following long term fight and a Demonstration of Congress, "Franklin Thompson" was found not guilty and granted an annuity in 1884.

In 1897, Edmonds was conceded into the Excellent Multitude of the Republic, the main lady part. After one year, on September 5, 1898, Edmonds kicked the bucket at her home in La Porte, Texas. In 1901, she was recovered with military distinctions at Washington Graveyard in Houston.

CHAPTER TWO
Sarah Emma Edmond As A Youth:

Edmonds was conceived on a homestead in New Brunswick, Canada in 1841, to Isaac Edmonds, of Scotland, and Elizabeth Leeper, of Ireland.

In her diary, Unsexed, or the Female Warrior, Sarah Edmonds expressed that her family was overprotective, causing her to feel "shielded however subjugated" and she depicted her dad as the "harsh speaker".

At the point when her dad attempted to wed her off to a neighbor at age 16, she fled from home, changed her name to Emma Edmonds and found a new line of work as a salesgirl in a millinery shop, as per the book, More Than Under skirts: Momentous Michigan Ladies:

"The milliner's shop was a position of harmony until her dad found her whereabouts. In 1858 Emma Edmonds fled once more. This time she changed more than her name. A long time later, subtleties of Emma's vanishing became known. She'd seen a notice for occupations selling books of scriptures and strict books, so Emma trim her hair, spent her investment funds on men's garments, and went after the position. She was employed and started her life as Plain Thompson."

Sarah Emma Edmonds in the Civil War:

In her journal, Edmonds expressed that while functioning as a book of scriptures sales rep in Stone, Michigan, she was sitting in a train station when she heard the report about the episode of the

Common War and realized she needed to make a move:

"I was stirred by my dream by a voice in the road crying 'New York Messenger – Fall of Fortress Sumter – President's Decree – Call for 75 thousand men!' This declaration surprised me, while my creative mind depicted the coming battle in the entirety of its dreadful extent... It is valid, I was not an American – I was not obliged to remain here during this awful hardship – I could revisit my local land where my folks would invite me to the home of my adolescence, and my siblings and sisters would celebrate my coming.

However, these were not the contemplations which consumed my psyche. It was not my aim, or want, to look for my very own simplicity and solace while so much distress constantly filled the land. In any case, the extraordinary inquiry to be chosen, was, what would I be able to do? What part am I to act in this extraordinary dramatization? I couldn't chose for myself – so I conveyed this inquiry to the Seat of Elegance and found a good answer there."

Simply a month later, on May 25, 1861, Edmonds joined as a male the field of nurture in the Second

Volunteers of the US Armed force under her nom de plume Franklin Rock Thompson.

Edmonds proceeded with her medical clinic work for a long time until Spring of 1862, when she was reassigned as a mail transporter for her regiment.

A couple of months after the fact, after one of General McClellan's government agents was gotten and executed by the Confederate armed force, Edmonds chipped in for the vacant situation, as she portrayed in her journals:

"In any case, would I say I was equipped for filling it with honor to myself and bit of leeway of the

Government? This was a significant inquiry for me to consider ere I continued further. I considered it altogether, and decided to acknowledge it with the entirety of its dreadful duties."

Edmonds wrote in her journal that her first covert agent mission included obscuring her skin with silver nitrate to act like a slave named "Sleeve" in a close by Confederate military camp.

While there, she helped fabricate defenses and worked in the kitchen where she listened in on discussions.

Edmonds got away a couple of days after the she was appointed as a Confederate picket and got back to reveal to McClellan himself of the data she accumulated on the Confederate neighborhood troop size, accessible weapons and area of various "Quaker Firearms"(logs painted to look like guns from a good ways) that the Confederates intended to use in Yorktown.

A couple of months after that, Edmonds said she invaded the Confederate armed force once more, this time as a female Irish vendor named Bridget O'Shea.

Edmonds got back from the outing with important military data just as a wonderful pony and an injury on her arm where the pony had bit her while she was recovering clinical supplies from the saddlebags.

After her regiment was moved to Virginia in 1862, Edmonds proceeded with her work as a covert agent, going secret again as "Sleeve"and later as an African American lady in a Confederate camp, a place that permitted her to take significant papers from official's coats which she took back to her regiment.

Edmonds expressed that she was available at numerous noteworthy fights, for example, the Skirmish of Antietam in September of 1862, during which she breast fed a mortally injured trooper who admitted to Edmonds that he was a really a lady in mask, as she stated in her diary.

"I tuned in with winded consideration regarding getting each solid which tumbled from those perishing lips, the substance of which was as per the following: 'I can believe you and will reveal to you a mystery. I am not what I appear, but rather am female. I enrolled from the most flawless intentions, and have stayed unfamiliar and unsuspected... I wish you to cover me with your own hands, that none may know after my passing that I am other than my appearance demonstrates.'... I stayed with her until she kicked the bucket, which was about 60 minutes. At that point making a grave for her under the shadow of a mulberry tree close to the war zone, aside from all the others, with the help of two of the young men who were definite to cover the dead, I conveyed her remaining parts to that forlorn spot and gave her an officer's entombment, without final resting place or cover, just a cover for a winding sheet. There she dozes in that lovely timberland where the delicate southern breezes murmur forlornly through the foliage, and the little winged animals sing pleasantly over her grave."

In the spring of 1863, Edmond's expressed that her regiment was moved to the multitude of Ulysses S. Award in anticipation of the Clash of Vicksburg.

It was around this time that Edmonds created jungle fever and ended up in a problem. Unfit to concede herself to a military clinic out of dread of being found, Edmonds chose to leave her unit and look for clinical consideration in a private emergency clinic.

In the wake of recuperating and leaving the emergency clinic in Cairo, Illinois, Edmonds saw a military announcement in the nearby mail center posting Private Blunt Thompson as a defector.

Incapable to revisit of her past obligations, Edmonds spent the remainder of the war filling in as a female attendant at emergency clinics in war torn districts like Virginia and West Virginia.

While working in Harper's Ship, Virginia, Edmonds met a single man from New Brunswick named Linus H. Seeyle and started a romance.

A few students of history question Edmonds stories and suspect she may have decorated reality to sell more duplicates of her journal, as per the book The Strange Private Thompson:

"The most sensational pieces of her book were her accounts of undercover work: the primary outing behind adversary lines at Yorktown, her adventures while dressed as an irish merchant lady, her fruitful surveillance while masked as a female slave during the Second Skirmish of Bull Run, and her emotional departure from the Confederate mounted force in Kentucky. These accounts were –

and are – difficult to check, however, valid or not, they added a lot of dramatization to the book, and are the wellspring of the suffering prevalent thinking that Emma was a government operative. There are likewise occasions that couldn't have happened to her since she was recorded to be elsewhere at that point. For instance, Emma's regiment was not at Antietam, yet she expounded on being there, and even incorporated an exaggerated story of the withering lady officer, so like Clara Barton's experience, which Emma may have heard or perused at that point. Emma likewise expounded on the attack at Vicksburg, which happened a while after she left the military, like she had been available. It is conceivable, in any case, that the hotspot for that material was [her friend] Jerome Robbins, who had been there and may have kept in touch with Emma about it."

CHAPTER THREE
Sarah Emma Edmonds After the Civil War:

In 1864, Edmonds distributed her diary, Unsexed, or The Female Warrior, which was later distributed under the titles The Female Covert operative of the Association Armed force, and The Attendant and Spy in the Association Armed force. The book immediately turned into a smash hit.

On April 27 of every 1867, Edmonds and Seeyle wedded at the Wendell House Lodging in Cleveland, Gracious and quickly moved back to Canada prior to getting back to the US where they traversed the U.S. looking for work, halting in Michigan, Ohio, Texas, Illinois, Louisiana and Kansas.

The couple lost three kids to ailment yet had two embraced two young men from a shelter Emma ran in Louisiana in the last part of the 1870s.

Still annoyed about being marked a miscreant and disturbed that she wasn't qualified for a benefits because of her sexual orientation, Edmonds appealed to the War Division for a full audit of her case. Different accounts of ladies who had served in battle were beginning to come out however none of them had at this point been granted an annuity.

Edmonds from the start attempted to conceal her actual character by applying for the vital evidence of her administration utilizing just her initials, S.E.E. Seeyle, on her administrative work however when the War Division kept on mentioning her complete name she chose to be forthright about her circumstance, as per the book The Strange Private Thompson:

"To that Aide Genl. Territory of Michigan my complete name is Sarah Emma Evelyn Seeyle. I enrolled and filled in as Franklin Thompson in Co 'F'second Mich Vols. Furthermore, allude you to Capt Damon Stewart of Stone Mich, Lieut Wm Turner of same, Capt Wm R Morse, Lawrence Kansas of Rock Mich, Gen O.M. Poe of Sherman's staff. I would state in the event that you would prefer not to give me the testament of administration simply say as much. Sarah Emma E. Seeyle."

Edmonds' confidants turned out in full help of her mission to get an annuity and talked profoundly of her during interviews and in their official oaths. Commander Morse later gave a meeting to the Kansas City Star in which he expressed:

"Franklin was known by each man in the regiment, and her abandonment was the subject of each open air fire. The clean shaven kid was a widespread top pick, and much uneasiness was communicated over her security. We never knew about her again during the war, and would never represent her departure."

However a portion of her different friends, for example, William Boston, expressed that there were gossipy tidbits up and down that Edmonds was a young lady and numerous in the regiment accepted she abandoned after a supposed sweetheart, an overseer in the military, surrendered.

Among the numerous affirmations for her situation document, Edmonds herself additionally presented a sworn explanation in which she attempted to dodge, for no good reason, affirming or denying her cases of reconnaissance she had expounded on in her journals:

"I offer no expression of any mystery administrations. In my brain there is nearly as much odious appendage to the word 'spy' as there is to the word 'defector.' There is so much mean duplicity essentially rehearsed by a government operative that I very much want everybody ought to accept that I never was past the foe's lines instead of to attach upon me by vow of a thing I scorn to such an extent. It might do in wartime, yet it isn't lovely to think upon in season of harmony."

In Spring of 1884, two bills were submitted to the Place of Delegates: one was to eliminate the charge of departure from Edmonds record and the other was to grant her a benefits of $12 every month. The report that went with the annuity bill expressed:

"Reality is ofttimes bizarre indeed, and now comes the spin-off, Sarah E. Edmonds, presently Sarah E. Seelye, moniker Franklin Thompson, is currently requesting this Congress to give her help by path from an annuity because of blurring wellbeing, which she asserts had its incurrence and is the succession of the days and evenings she spent in the bogs of the Chickahominy in the days she spent soldiering. That Franklin

Thompson and Mrs. Sarah E.E. Seelye are very much the same individual is set up by plenitude of confirmation and without question. She presents an assertion . . . and furthermore the declaration of ten solid observers, men of insight, holding spots of high honor and trust, who decidedly swear she is the indistinguishable Franklin Thompson. . . ."

On July 5 of 1884, a Unique Demonstration of Congress at long last allowed Edmonds a veteran's benefits of $12 every month except the bill to demonstrate her innocence moved gradually and wasn't passed until July of 1886.

She at that point needed to apply for the compensation and abundance she would have acquired on the off chance that she wasn't accused of abandonment, a cycle which took an additional two years.

Since her case created a ton of exposure, Edmonds became something of a big name in her humble community of Fortification Scott and was granted participation into the Common War veterans association, the Excellent Multitude of the Republic, in 1897.

In the fall of 1897, Edmonds became sick with another episode of intestinal sickness and in spite of the fact that she began to recuperate a couple of months after the fact, before the finish of the mid year she was experiencing loss of motion potentially welcomed on by a stroke.

Edmonds died on September 5, 1898 and was covered in a nearby burial ground in La Porte, Texas. In 1901, Edmonds was recovered with military distinctions at Washington Burial ground in Houston.

CHAPTER FOUR

Sarah Emma Edmonds - Civil War Warrior, Spy, and Medical caretaker

Envisioned as a government agent whose mission was to go behind adversary lines camouflaged as an Individual of color or an Irish seller lady to assemble data during the American Common War. There was such a covert agent, and it was anything but a man, or an American besides. The covert agent's name was Sarah Emma Edmonds, conceived in Magaguadavic, New Brunswick in 1841. What is much more unordinary is that her kindred warriors didn't realize that she was a lady; they all idea her name was Forthright Thompson.

Sarah Emma Edmonds spent the American Common War camouflaged as an officer named Franklin Thompson. Truth be told, she had consumed quite a bit of her time on earth concealing her actual character. Edmonds ventured out from home in 1857, clearly getting away from a damaging dad and the danger of an orchestrated marriage. In when ladies voyaging alone was not just disapproved of, also hazardous, Sarah embraced the persona of Franklin Thompson to travel simpler and work without inconvenience. For a couple of years she ventured to every part of the Oceanic regions selling Books of scriptures. And afterward the Common War started. Sarah was attracted to experience and this war made certain to be the extraordinary experience that she looked for.

Edmonds emigrated to the U.S., and on May 25, 1861, she enrolled in Organization F of the second Michigan Infantry, otherwise called the Rock Association Grays. Broad actual assessments were not needed for selection at that point, and she was not found. She from the outset filled in as a male field nurture, taking an interest in a few missions under Broad McClellan, including the First and Second Skirmish of Bull Run, Antietam, the Promontory Lobby, Vicksburg, Fredericksburg, and others.

Edmonds' vocation took a turn during the war when an Association spy in Richmond,

Virginia was found and went before a terminating crew, and a companion, James Vesey, was slaughtered in a snare. She exploited the open spot and the occasion to retaliate for her companion's passing. She applied for, and won, the situation as Franklin Thompson.

Heading out into hostile area to accumulate data required Emma to think of numerous masks. One camouflage required Edmonds to utilize silver nitrate to color her skin dark, wear a dark hairpiece, and stroll into the Alliance masked as a person of color by the name of Sleeve. Some other time she entered as an Irish seller lady by the name of Bridget O'Shea, guaranteeing that she was offering apples and cleanser to the troopers. Once more, she was "working for the Confederates"as a dark laundress when a parcel of authentic papers dropped out of an official's coat. At the point when Thompson got back to the Association with the papers, the commanders were pleased. Some other time, she filled in as an investigator in Maryland as Charles Mayberry, finding a specialist for the Alliance.

Edmonds' profession as Forthright Thompson reached a conclusion when she contracted intestinal sickness. She relinquished her obligation in the military, expecting that in the event that she went to a military emergency clinic she would be found. She took a look at herself into a private emergency clinic, meaning to revisitation of military life whenever she had recovered. When she recuperated, notwithstanding, she saw banners posting Blunt Thompson as a coward. Instead of revisitation of the military under another false name or as Straightforward Thompson, gambling execution for abandonment, she chose to fill in as a female attendant at a Washington, D.C. medical clinic for injured troopers.

Her kindred fighters commended her military help, and even after her camouflage was found, thought of her as a decent trooper. She was alluded to as a valiant officer and was dynamic in each fight her regiment confronted.

In 1864 Edmonds' record of her military encounters were distributed as "Medical caretaker and Spy in the Association Armed force". A resonating achievement, Edmonds gave the benefits from her diary to "different fighters' guide association."

Sarah got back to New Brunswick in 1867 and wedded woodworker Linus Seelye. They had three youngsters who kicked the bucket youthful and they embraced two young men. Sarah appealed to the War Office for an audit of her case. On July 5, 1884 Congress allowed Sarah a respectable release from the military just as a veteran's benefits of $12 per month. She passed on of intestinal sickness in 1898 and was covered with full military distinctions in Washington Burial ground in Houston, Texas. She is the main female standard individual from the Terrific Multitude of the

Republic, an association shaped after the Common Battle by Association veterans.

THE END

Made in the USA
Middletown, DE
30 September 2021